Robert Quackenbush

QUICK, ANNIE, GIVE ME A CATCHY LINE!

A STORY OF SAMUEL F.B. MORSE

Prentice-Hall, Inc.

Copyright © 1983 by Robert Quackenbush
Published by Prentice-Hall Books for Young Readers
A Division of Simon & Schuster, Inc.
Simon & Schuster Building
Rockefeller Center
1230 Avenue of the Americas
New York, NY 10020

10 9 8 7 6 5 4 3 2

10 9 8 7 6 5 4 3 2 1 pbk

Prentice-Hall Books for Young Readers
is a trademark of Simon & Schuster, Inc.
Manufactured in the United States of America

Library of Congress Cataloging in Publication Data

Quackenbush, Robert M.
   Quick, Annie, give me a catchy line!

   Summary: A brief biography of the inventor of the
world's first practical telegraph system.
   1. Morse, Samuel Finley Breese, 1791-1872 —
Juvenile literature.   2. Inventors — United States —
Biography — Juvenile literature.   [1. Morse, Samuel
Finley Breese, 1791-1872.   2. Inventors]   I. Title.
TK5243.M7Q33   1983   621.382'092'4 [B] [92]   82-21462
ISBN 0-13-749762-8

Samuel Finley Breese Morse, born in 1791 in Charlestown, Massachusetts, never did what he was expected to do. While his two younger brothers pored over books like their highly educated father and grandfather, young Samuel would be doing something else. Even when he was sent, in his father's footsteps, at age fourteen to attend college at Yale, Morse kept out of the mainstream. While everyone around him was busy with schoolwork, Morse was dreaming that class was over so he could go painting, drawing, and sketching. Science was about the only subject that held his interest.

9

Morse liked science because it was a subject that had just been introduced to American colleges. He was fascinated by some of the classroom experiments. He took apart and reassembled the first kind of battery that had been invented; it contained copper and zinc discs and chemicals that worked together to produce electricity. He also learned about another invention that could store a charge of electricity. It was called a Leyden jar. When the class joined hands in a circle around the jar and the lead man touched the top while the end man touched the side, everyone, simultaneously, received a shock. This proved that electricity flowed in an instantaneous current. But this was about the only "charge" Morse got out of his college days. When he left Yale, at nineteen, he had not prepared himself for a profession.

11

Morse thought it over and decided he wanted to be an artist. But it was a profession that was almost unheard of in those days. The country was new and most people were poor, so paintings were considered a luxury. Only a few people could earn a living by painting pictures. This did not stop Morse. He went to see two of America's finest painters, Gilbert Stuart and Washington Allston. The two masters thought Morse's work was good; they convinced his parents that he might find a place for himself in the art world. With that, Morse went off with Allston to study in Europe. Four years later, in 1815, he returned to exhibit a group of "history" paintings in Boston. One giant painting, entitled "Dying Hercules," showed the mythical hero lying in agony against a rock. The public would have none of Morse's pictures. Now what was he going to do?

To earn a living, Morse turned to painting portraits. He was not thrilled about doing them, but people seemed to want them. After a few jobs came his way, he settled down and got married. Before long a child was born, and then another. About the time a third child was due, Morse was having trouble finding enough portraits to paint in Boston to support his rapidly growing family. So he sent his wife and children to live with his parents while he took to the road. He went to Albany, New York City, and Charleston, South Carolina, in search of portraits to paint.

15

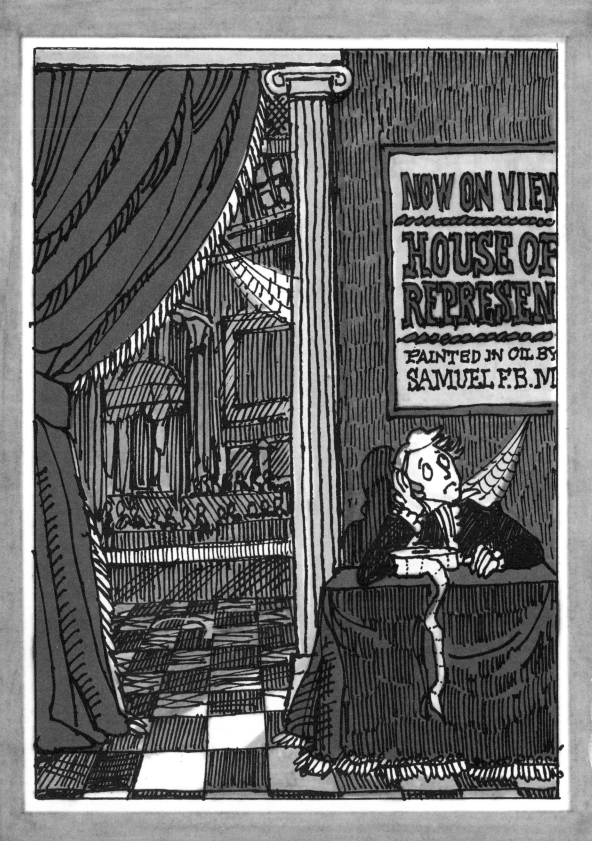

By now, twenty years had gone by, and Morse was still struggling to find a rewarding career in art. It was true that he had painted brilliant portraits of Eli Whitney, Daniel Webster, and the Marquis de Lafayette—to name a few. But the portrait commissions didn't come often enough, and when they did they didn't pay enough. And it was also true that he had founded and was head of the National Academy of Design at a time when there were no art galleries, much less art schools, in New York. But this didn't pay, either. He tried all kinds of ways to make money with his art. One time he charged admission for the people of New York to see a giant portrait of Congress he had painted. No one came. In desperation, he decided that a return trip to Europe might change his luck. It didn't. A huge canvas he painted in Paris called "The Gallery of the Louvre," showing dozens of famous paintings mounted on the museum's walls, brought only snubs. Morse headed back home.

17

THE JUNK PASSENGERS BRING ON BOARD THESE DAYS!

YOU CAN SAY THAT AGAIN.

SULLY

Returning to the United States in 1832 aboard the packet ship *Sully*, Morse had a conversation in the dining saloon one night that changed his life. A young doctor, Charles T. Jackson, explained how electricity could travel like fluid for miles and miles over a wire. At once Morse was struck with an idea. He could see no reason why a message could not be instantaneously sent over a wire to any distance by electricity. He believed he could invent an instrument to send and receive such messages. He would call it an electric telegraph. For the rest of the voyage he could talk of nothing else. He drove his fellow passengers crazy with his endless talk about an electric telegraph and a code he had devised for it. The code was an alphabet of dots and dashes that could be printed or sounded on a buzzer by opening or closing an electric circuit. But what Morse did not know was that Professor Joseph Henry, a noted physicist, had demonstrated an electric telegraph system in Albany, New York, the year before. In fact, Henry had even published a paper about it.

19

Joseph Henry had demonstrated his telegraph system by stringing a mile of wire around his classroom. At one end he attached a sending device, or transmitter, hooked up to a battery. At the other end was an iron bar wrapped in wire, called an electromagnet. When the transmitter caused an electric current to go from the battery through the wire to magnetize the bar, the bar caused a permanent magnet to swing on a pivot and ring a small bell. This was the first electromagnetic telegraph. But Henry was more interested in research than in commercial ventures, so he did not bother to have his telegraph patented. This made it possible for Morse to set to work inventing an electromagnetic telegraph of his own. His reason for wanting to invent one was simple. He hoped it would make him rich so he could devote the rest of his life to painting without a worry or care. He did not stop to think that he was going from one impractical profession to another. But that was Morse for you!

Morse didn't start working on his telegraph right away. One cause for delay was his decision to run for mayor of New York. He campaigned against almost everything! (Morse's political ideas would seem unacceptable to most people today.) He lost that election and soon ran in another. When he lost the second time, he finally went back to his telegraph and to teaching art at New York University. He built his telegraph out of old canvas stretchers, wooden clock parts, and whatever else he could find around his studio. When it was finished, he energized the system. But it just lay there. Morse poked at this wire and wiggled that one. Still nothing happened. Finally, he begged one of the physicists at the university, Professor Leonard Gale, to take a look at it. Gale was flabbergasted. Morse had wrapped bare uninsulated wire around his magnets. Gale showed him how the magnet and batteries ought to work. He also suggested that Morse study Joseph Henry's published article. Morse needed all the help he could get. So on the spot he took Gale on as a partner.

After making the changes Gale suggested and finding out that his telegraph could work, Morse took on a new partner, Alfred Vail. Vail, a former student at the university, agreed to help Morse improve his invention in exchange for one fourth of the profits it would earn. The final result was a machine that was similar to Henry's in principle; however, it could send messages much greater distances. It had what is called a relay. This was an electric battery on the line that would add to the current every time a signal was being sent by a transmitter. This boosted the signal along to a receiver, where it was either transformed to a rat-tat-tat sound or printed on a strip of paper. The message that came out of the receiver, whether it was audible or printed, represented dots and dashes. In turn, these dots and dashes represented letters of the alphabet and became known as the Morse Code.

25

Morse's dedication to the telegraph took more and more time away from his art, until, in 1836, he put down his brushes forever. Two years later, in February 1838, he was invited to give a demonstration of his electric telegraph before the House Committee on Commerce in Washington, D.C. It created a sensation. The committee chairman, Congressman F.O.J. Smith, became Morse's third partner in the telegraph. His task was to launch a bill in Congress that would grant Morse $30,000 to build fifty miles of telegraph. Elated, Morse set sail for Europe to patent his telegraph in as many foreign countries as possible. But he did not have much luck because a telegraph that had been invented by an Englishman, Sir Charles Wheatstone, was already in use in Europe.

27

Morse returned to the United States broke and hungry. He wondered if Congress would *ever* pass his bill. To earn money, he began a new trade he had learned in Europe. He became a teacher of the daguerreotype—one of the earliest forms of photography, made by exposing an image on a plate of chemically treated metal or glass. One of his students was the great Mathew Brady, who years later would become famous for his photographs of the Civil War. But this, too, did not bring in much money, and Morse remained terribly poor. A story is told that when one of his students got behind in his payments, Morse asked when he would be paid. The student answered that he would be paid in one week. Morse replied that he would be dead by then. Quickly, the student rushed Morse out for a meal before it was too late!

29

Five more years passed. Morse was still waiting for Congress to pass his bill. If the bill failed, he knew he would be ruined. At last, in February 1843, Congress planned to bring his bill to a vote. Morse checked into a Washington hotel and waited. By the last day of the congressional session, there was still no word. Morse crawled into bed that night knowing that he had just enough money to pay his hotel bill and his train fare back to New York. The next morning there was a knock on his door. Annie Ellsworth, the daughter of a friend, brought Morse tremendous news. Congress had passed his bill 89 to 83, and at midnight President Pierce had signed it! Beside himself with joy, Morse told Annie she could choose the first message that would be sent over his electric telegraph. After some thought, she chose, "What hath God wrought?"

The test telegraph line was planned to run right alongside the railroad tracks that stretched forty miles between Washington and Baltimore. The wire was placed in lead pipes and installed underground. But there were problems. It was discovered after nine miles that the electricity would leak from the wire into the ground. The underground operation had to be halted. Morse had spent $23,000 of the money from Congress. There was only $7,000 left. The only thing he could think of was to attach the wire to poles. Twenty-four-foot-tall unbarked chestnut poles were put up every two hundred feet along the tracks. And to save more money, Morse used broken bottle necks at the top of each pole for insulators. On May 24, 1844, the telegraph line was finished, and Annie Ellsworth's message went from Washington to Baltimore. Morse's electromagnetic telegraph was a success!

At first, neither Morse nor anyone else knew what to do with the telegraph. But it seemed to take over, in spite of itself. Before long a line was laid across the Atlantic Ocean. Soon a cobweb of Morse's wires covered the world. His telegraph replaced all others—even Wheatstone's, which failed because it made no sound. And so a man who knew hardly anything about electricity and even less about mechanics succeeded in giving the world a practical telegraph system—and got rich at last. After several patent battles over claims by rival inventors, fights with partners, angry quarrels with Professor Henry and with Doctor Jackson, Morse was given full legal credit for inventing the telegraph and was ready to settle down and enjoy his fame and wealth. Ready, that is, but not willing. He could never be like other people, and he drifted back to his absurd politics and other silly pursuits. But that was Morse for you.

35

ᡣᢙ EPILOGUE ᢙᡓ

Many inventors, particularly Joseph Henry, contributed to the invention of the electric telegraph. But it was Morse who had enough determination, interest, and persistence to sell a new device to an indifferent public. For over forty years his telegraph was the world's most important means of long-distance communication. Then came the telephone, the radio, and finally today's satellite TV, which have dimmed the importance of the telegraph. Even so, the name of Samuel F. B. Morse continues to shine for another reason. Today, after nearly one hundred and fifty years, Morse's paintings and portraits are famous, and people across the land flock to see special exhibits of his work at museums and galleries. And the final irony involves "The Gallery of the Louvre," the painting that was ignored by the public in 1832. It was sold by the University of Syracuse in 1982 for the astounding figure of $3,500,000—the highest sum yet paid for an American painter's work.